*To every thing there is a season,
and a time to every purpose under the heaven.*

ECCLESIASTES 3:1 KJV

PRESENTED TO:

Amber & family

FROM:

Sheila Seborg

DATE:

Feb. 27, 2000

Seasons of the Heart

A CELEBRATION OF LOVE BETWEEN
MOTHERS AND DAUGHTERS

By

Ginny Hobson and Sherry Morris

Seasons of the Heart:
A Celebration of Love Between Mothers and Daughters
ISBN 1-56292-491-5
Copyright © 1998 by Ginny Hobson and Sherry Morris
The Carpentree
P. O. Box 100
Tulsa, Oklahoma 74101

Published by Honor Books
P. O. Box 55388
Tulsa, Oklahoma 74155

*This book is dedicated to our mothers and daughters
and to our grandmothers, who passed their heritage to us
so we can offer it to the next generation:*

to Virginia, mother to both of us,
to Sherry's mother, Marilyn, now gone,
to Jennifer, Katie, and Kelly, our girls, big and little,
to Aunt Carolyn and Aunt Fran, who are like a mother to each of us,
to Grammy, Nana, Grandma Weaver, and Grandma Floyd—
we will always remember the love you gave us.

*And to mothers and daughters everywhere—
May you celebrate the seasons of your heart always.*

Acknowledgments

We would like to acknowledge and thank our husbands and children for their help and patience while they endured missed meals and messy paper trails. We love you all, Dan, Daniel, Jordan, Steve, Katie, Adam, and Kelly.

Thanks to you, our dear friends Carrie, Rosalind, Martha, Jadine, Charity, and Ginny's daughter Jennifer, who added your own special memories from each season of your heart. Our heartfelt thanks goes to our editor, Sue Rhodes Sesso, for her encouragement and prayerful support. And we especially thank Honor Books and Bob Zaloba, who gave us encouragement and direction in giving birth to this labor of love.

The Canvas of Her Heart

The beauty in artist Glynda Turley's life is painted against a background of color from generations past. Her story of her mother and grandmother paints in rich detail the legacy these women gave to Glynda at a young age.

As a nationally acclaimed artist, Glynda is loved for her gift of creativity and artistic style that touches the hearts of many. As did her mother and grandmother before her, she uses her artistry to bring joy to her family, friends, and now collectors of her work. The canvas of her heart written here also has many treasures for each of us to enjoy.

Table of Contents

Celebrating the Seasons

In every heart there are memories that leave their mark on our lives. Pressed like cherished flowers between the pages of a family album, some of these memories are tattered with age and faded by the passage of time. Others are as fresh as a bloom just lovingly placed in our book of shared memories. These experiences shape who we are as mothers and daughters. Like a family takes an album off the shelf to reminisce about days gone by, mothers and daughters need to take time to look into seasons of the past and celebrate the moments of life that make each of us who we are.

Slowly, the seasons of the year turn, and the relationship between mother and daughter changes. In the circle of the seasons, memories become the markers that define who we are as mothers and daughters. Filled with days of sunshine and shadow, with color and intensity that span the spectrum of life from pale to vibrant, the passing of events into yesterday compels both mother and daughter to examine their book of shared memories. Seasons of the heart begin like the spring, full of hope and promise. Then, as time passes, this unique relationship turns from tender bud to full flower, from a gentle shower to a flood of emotion, and from warm thoughts to cool undercurrents, and back again. If care is taken to nurture hearts and protect them through the tumultuous seasons, the bonding of kindred hearts warms and brightens our lives no matter what the climate of our days.

From pages kept carefully in our book of memories, our lives are organized into seasons of the heart. For a while, the images of past days are tossed haphazardly into our lives. Sometimes the busyness of living keeps the roots of intimacy shallow between mothers and daughters. There is little time or energy to explore our feelings, to share our thoughts, or to examine just how much mother and daughter influence each other. At some point in our lives, if we are wise, we should begin to reflect, to restore, and to carefully arrange the past into some order that will help us understand the people we are today. Reflecting on past experiences of being a mother and daughter brings the hope that the future will reveal an even stronger bond of closeness. Understanding the seasons of the heart is a journey into yesterday that casts a silhouette on tomorrow.

Each of us is on a journey through life that is unique and special. Beginning with the gentle season of spring, mothers and daughters plant the first seeds in what will become one of the most significant relationships in their lives. Following the spring, the more intense rays of summer sometimes leave us thirsty for deeper roots of understanding. With the coming of autumn, the winds of change in the relationship begin to blow. Winter, the season of serenity, is covered in a blanket of warm and loving reflections. Each season of the heart is filled with special joys and, sometimes, a few regrets.

We invite you to come with us on a journey through *Seasons of the Heart*. As you travel along through the stories that follow, we hope you will open an album of your own special memories. May each of you, as a mother or a daughter, share with each other the seasons of your heart so that these quickly passing measures of time will be forever remembered.

—GINNY HOBSON AND SHERRY MORRIS

Seasons of the Heart

Spring

Lo, children are an heritage of the Lord.

PSALM 127:3 KJV

A time to be born . . . a time to plant

Spring is the emerging season. From the earth, the garden springs and flowers bud, opening with both color and fragrance, filling the senses with wonder and delight. From the skies, birds begin their happy song and dance of spring. They sing their sweet notes into a heart-lifting melody.

A more subtle beginning is not so evident to the senses. It springs not from the ground or the skies. From the heart emerges a feeling, a state of being that is both complex and nurturing. Its happy wonder occupies our days and its sweet music fills our minds. Enriching our lives as women, the heart reveals a time and a place within where we can find—and cherish—a relationship that will color the rest of our days.

It is in the springtime that a woman first experiences the delight of a baby's chuckle, the treasure of peanut butter sandwich picnics in the park, and both the excitement and "butterflies in the tummy" of her child's first day of school. Yet, with the joys come the difficulties of late-night feedings, too little sleep, and a myriad of other distresses and frustrations. Both the agony and the ecstasy of motherhood are experienced moment by moment. Lullabies and rocking chairs, bedtime stories and tea parties, and sandbox afternoons and trips to the zoo slip unobtrusively into the past. These lovely days are replaced by carpools and music lessons. Almost imperceptibly, this gentle season passes. The next season will arrive too soon.

During the springtime of our hearts as mothers, it seems as if we are each given a paintbrush. With this brush we begin to stroke—intentionally or otherwise—the intensity of color and the degree of warmth that will define our relationships with our daughters. With each brush stroke, a story is born. Springtime in a mother's heart is the beginning of a lifelong journey throughout the seasons.

Waiting for Amy

MARTHA MEEKS
(AS TOLD TO SHERRY MORRIS)

While Martha was still in high school, she met a young woman who had adopted a Korean baby. She knew at the time the event was significant in her life. Even at 17, Martha felt that God placed a desire in her heart to adopt. She asked her new friend many questions about the process. She even contacted the agency that assisted in the adoption of her friend's baby. They gave her a brochure about their agency. Martha kept it all through college. Before she and her husband Scott were married, she told him of her desire to adopt a Korean child. After her boys were born, she finally threw away the adoption agency brochure.

Because Martha had always thought God was preparing her to adopt rather than give birth, it almost surprised her that she conceived and gave birth so easily. Three healthy, active boys should have been enough to complete her family. Yet, she wondered what it would be like to have a little girl. As she dressed her boys in overalls and sneakers, she thought how nice it would be to dress a daughter in lace and ribbons. As the boys played games inspired by the latest superhero action figures, Martha wished for a girl to have a tea party with in the afternoons. Watching Scott and the boys wrestling on the living room floor, she wondered what it would be like to have a daughter. It would be nice to have someone else in the house who was interested in shopping and talking, instead of roughhousing and playing ball.

After some time passed, Martha became aware that she still felt a strong yearning to see her dream realized. When she finally had the courage to reveal her thoughts and feelings to Scott, she was elated that he also felt that their family was missing someone. His heart had also traveled across the sea to the land of Korea, where a little girl was waiting for a family.

When a young woman carries a child within her, it may seem that nine months is a long time to wait for something so precious and wonderful as a baby. For the mother who is waiting to adopt a child, the wait can be much more than nine months, even stretching to years, before she feels the joy of cradling the little one she longs for in her arms. For Martha, waiting for Amy seemed like an eternity. In a journal she has kept for her daughter, Martha describes both the elation and the agony she experienced until the day she took Amy from a social worker's arms and held her for the first time.

NOVEMBER 5

Dear little Amy,

Where do I begin? I know in my heart God began preparing me for you when I was 17 years old. Now, all these years later, our whole family waits for you. Your daddy and I began the process of adopting you in July. We have done pages and pages of paperwork, been checked out by doctors, sent fingerprints to the FBI, and been interviewed by several caseworkers. Guess what? We passed. We have been approved! Now the hard part begins. We have to wait for you. It could be as long as a year. A year! I am so ready to hold you in my arms now. Your daddy and I and your brothers Chris, Sam, and Ben are impatient, too. Ben is ready to help take care of you. Sam is ready to give you hugs and kisses. Chris just can't understand why his baby isn't here yet. He wants to teach you everything.

Your daddy and I are praying for you and for your Korean mom. She loves you, too. It must be hard for her to know she must let you go. We pray that God will give her peace and reassurance that you will be a cherished and important part of a new family.

I dreamed last night that I was in the hospital where you were born. A woman handed you to me and said, "Here is your Amy." As I took you from her, you wrinkled up your tiny little newborn face and started to cry. Then, I kissed your soft little cheek and put your head on my shoulder. Immediately you were quiet and you buried your soft face into my neck and slept.

Oh, Amy! You felt so real! Although I know I can't be with you when you are born, I feel like I have held you. It's a dream I believe was a gift and a promise from God. Your name will be Amy (the beloved) and Elise (promise of God).

We love you. *Mommy*

Seasons of the Heart

JANUARY 10

Ja (merciful) Young (glorious)—You are ours now! Oh, sweet Amy you were born in August! We saw a video of you and have seen pictures. We prayed that God would bring us news of you this week! We know you belong to us! We have no doubts. God made you, Ja Young, and knew you would be part of our family.

Daddy and I are so happy and busy doing all we can to bring you home to us and to get ready for you. When we told your brothers you were coming home soon, they cheered, danced, and smiled! Your big brother, Ben has wanted a baby sister since he was two years old. When he realized that the precious little girl on the video was his baby sister, he cried. Tears of joy!

When I had the dream I was holding you in the hospital, it was the same day your foster mother put you in the hospital because you were sick with pneumonia. We have the hospital records to show it. I believe that in God's incredible way, I was holding you that night, and somehow you felt me there comforting you, too. It won't be too long.

I love you. *Mom*

MARCH 21

I thought it would not be long until I held you. I was wrong in two ways. First, the eight weeks we expected to wait has grown to nearly eleven and counting. I also could not have predicted how much it hurts to wait for you— how desperately I want to hold you! I did not know how slowly time would seem to pass. Sometimes I cry because I want you so much. Daddy tries to cheer me up, and your brothers give me extra hugs, but they all want you now, too! Everything has been ready for you for a long time now. The baby shower (weeks ago) was wonderful. Your room is painted and ready. Even the high chair is waiting for you!

We miss you. We love you. Come home soon. *Mommy*

14

APRIL 16

Amy, you are home! You came to us nine days ago. Life with you is wonderful. There is no doubt that you were chosen by God and placed in our family. You fit perfectly!

The phone rang just after 9:00 a.m., March 31. It was the adoption agency telling me you had flight plans. You would arrive in Los Angeles on April 7. I hung up the phone shaking with joy.

Daddy and I flew to Los Angeles the night before you arrived. The next morning we drove to the airport to meet you. We held hands and prayed for your safe arrival. The adoption agency had told us to allow two hours between when you arrived and when we boarded another plane to take you home. Your plane was an hour late. We were nervous but had hope in prayer. The flight arrival terminal showed yet another 20-minute delay. Finally, your plane landed but did not have room to pull into the gate. More than two hours late, you came off the plane with the social worker who traveled with you. You were crying. I was crying. You were still on the other side of a glass wall and had to pass through customs before I could hold you. Our plane home was about to board. Still, we waited for you. At last, a frantic social worker ran through the door and handed you to me saying only, "Run!" We turned away and ran to the other side of the airport, and we made our plane! Out of breath and overwhelmed with emotion, we sat in our seats and got to see you for the first time. It was a great feeling. You cried just a bit (who could blame you!) and then you slept. We watched your little face and took turns snuggling you in our arms. Daddy counted your fingers and your toes. Over the intercom, the flight attendant announced, "Congratulations to Amy and her new parents!"

When you first came home, you were very weak. But in nine days you have made great progress. Although you are 7½ months already, we are watching you grow and learn to do things we thought we would miss. Yesterday, you sat alone for the first time. You make us smile. Amy Flise, you are beloved and you are the fulfilled promise of God for our family.

Love, *Your Very Happy and Joyful Mom*

The Gift of You

JENNIFER HOBSON LAMB

I close my eyes and know
That in my mind I'll always be able to
See your precious face,
Hear your soft "coo's,"
And smell your baby fresh skin.
I'm holding a part of me.
It's not just my physical or character traits you have—
It's my heart.

From the moment they placed you in my arms,
My love for you overflowed immeasurably.
How is it that I was chosen to be given such a great reward?
No certificate, no degree, no promotion or praise,
Can compare to you—
The gift of life.

How incredible to take part in a miracle with God.
Even as you grew inside of me,
I truly began to understand just how precious life is.
My child, you captivate my emotions,
And provide me with an endless source of joy.

I anxiously anticipate each milestone you will make,
But yet I know I must savor each moment,
Because they pass so quickly.
I realize you will not always be so tiny and fragile,
And I know you will not always be so dependent on me.

I wonder what I did with my time before you?
What could compare to
Seeing your first smile,
Hearing your delightful "coo's,"
Watching you "discover" your fingers,
Realizing you recognize my face and voice,
Feeling your precious hand grasp my finger,
Nestling your tiny head on my shoulder as I carry you,
Holding you close and feeling your tired little body rest on mine,
Singing songs to you as we rock-a-bye and all our cares just fade away.
Yes, you've realigned my priorities,
I now understand the importance of cherishing the present,
Forgetting the past and not worrying about the future.
I now realize that perfection isn't what matters—
It's having peace in your heart and home.

I can now see that true prosperity is not defined by the material,
But by the eternal.
I'm learning that where my treasure is,
There will my heart be also.

My child—
My arms will hold you,
My mind will teach you,
My heart will always love you.

As I stand over your cradle once again,
And watch you so intently,
I am in awe of the miracle of life—
Enriched by your presence,
And thankful to God
For blessing me with the gift of you.

I Love You 4 . . . ever

SUE RHODES SESSO

*On my daughter's birthday every year, we have a tradition of remembering all the details
of her entrance into this world. All day long, I give her a blow-by-blow description
of what I was experiencing on the day of her birth. She is a teenager now and never tires
of hearing the mini-episodes of our story. In fact, her birthday simply
would not be complete without this tradition. At certain times of the day,
I look at my watch and announce the time of day and share a memory.*

"It' s 7:05 a.m. I'm feeling strange little flutters. I've heard that contractions are supposed to be long and hard, and I convince myself that these gentle little ripples are nothing. Nothing. Nothing at all.

"It's 8:30 a.m., and my mother is lining the front seat with plastic bags and towels in the unlikely event that my water would break on the way to the doctor's office. I roll my eyes at her extravagant tendency to prepare for every possible disaster and hoist myself into the car. As I strap on the seatbelt, I remember the phone number list of friends and family who should be notified if the baby arrives today. My mother hops out of the car to fetch the list, and as she closes the door, I am instantly grateful for mom's new car interior damage control. My water breaks, and all doubt that those strange little flutters could not possibly be the onset of labor is totally dispelled.

"It's almost noon, and the doctor has confirmed that 'this is it, folks,' and we notify family and friends of your impending delivery. As the day progresses, I ponder whether you will be a girl or a boy. I can't help myself. Every time I think of my baby, it is a *she* wearing ribbons and lace.

"Four hours later, I am in hard labor, but no baby. The doctor decides to let me go for another hour or so while he closely monitors the situation. Soon he orders diagnostic X-rays. Within the hour, it is apparent that in order to save mother and child, a C-section is necessary.

"At 7:39 p.m., I hear this woeful wail as you make your entrance into the world. My eyes still well up with tears every time I remember the moment you were born. I don't suppose the angels were *actually* singing, but it just felt that way to me. The rush of joy and wonder and awe and happiness I felt at your birth remains one of my cherished lifetime memories. Wonder of wonders, if you are the only child I ever have, God gave me the daughter I wanted so badly.

"It's around 9 p.m., and everyone has heard the good news of your arrival and rushed to the hospital to get their first glimpse of you. I want to be the one who announces your name to our family. I watch my mother as I say your name for the first time. She looks surprised and then smiles with tears in her eyes. I have honored her and given you a special gift in my choice. Your name says that you are a part of our family history. Your first name is my middle name and also belongs to my aunt and grandmother. You share your middle name with your aunt in heaven, your grandmother, her grandmother, and her great-great aunt."

As it turned out, my Lili is, indeed, the only child I have. I watch this precious blessing that God has entrusted into my care grow and blossom from a bubbly toddler into a bright and beautiful young woman. We try to savor every moment together as the sweet gift it is. And some of our traditions have become wonderful memories we will cherish for the rest of our lives.

Even now at bedtime, after talks and laughter and hugs and kisses and prayers, we seem to always say our final goodnight the same way:

"I love you, Mom."

"I love you, too."

With a look of mischief, Lili responds, "I love you 3."

We smile and say our last line together, "I love you 4 . . . ever."

Seasons of the Heart

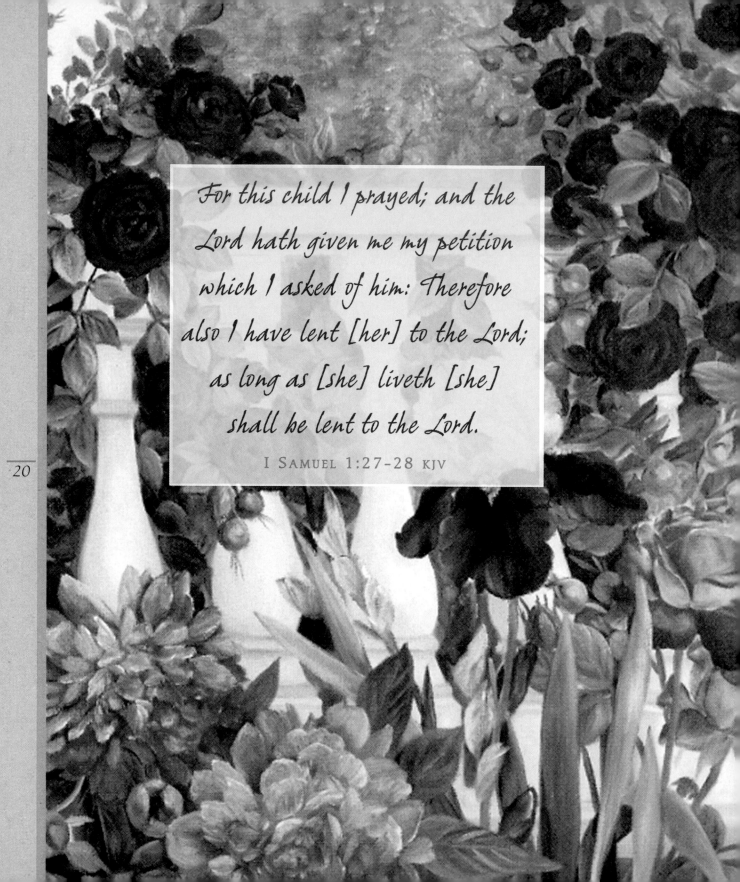

For this child I prayed; and the Lord hath given me my petition which I asked of him: Therefore also I have lent [her] to the Lord; as long as [she] liveth [she] shall be lent to the Lord.

I SAMUEL 1:27–28 KJV

20

Little Girls Just Take Time

GINNY HOBSON

Children are a gift from God
for man and wife together,
and if we will take the time
this gift will last forever.

For it just takes time to talk of God,
to show them how to pray,
And it takes time to plant in them
the joy of each new day.

It just takes time to listen
to all their dreams and plans,
And to help them build once more
when their castles turn to sand.

It just takes time to teach them
to know the wrong from right,
and it takes time to wipe their brow
and to stay up half the night.

It just takes time to comfort them
when the other team has won,
to let them know to mom and dad
they'll still be "number one."

It just takes time to watch them sing
on some elementary stage,
Even though they're just in the chorus
and not really in the play.

It just takes time to tell them
that you love them every day.
To hold and scold and comfort them
as you guide them on their way.

It just takes time to say "no"
when they cry and plead and beg,
and it takes time to read to them
when you say, "It's time for bed."

Yes, it does take time to hold their hands
when they take their first few steps,
and it takes great time to let them go
when they want to leave the nest.

This love we show to our little girls
never costs one single dime;
yet the memories we have last forever
and all we spend is time.

21

What Mother Learned the Day Katie Went to Kindergarten

SHERRY MORRIS

*Inherent to motherhood is a conflicting set of emotions. On the one hand,
there is the rational and sane desire to raise independent, self-reliant children.
On the other hand, there is, in the heart of all mothers at least some of the time,
the deeply felt "need to be needed." It sometimes rises from the depth
of a mother's heart, rippling the waters and creating a surface tension
that together mother and daughter have to learn to traverse. For me, the first ripple on
the water came when my daughter's journey toward independence
took her out of my house and onto a bus for her first day at kindergarten.*

Katie was up before I was, asking for her breakfast, checking and rechecking her book bag to make sure her new school supplies were still in the bag and hurrying me through my first cup of coffee. She usually required several calls or a crane to pull her from her bed. Somehow she managed to dress herself on time and stand at the front door ready to go.

Slowly I drank my coffee while she waited impatiently by the door. I thought to myself that Katie couldn't possibly be ready for kindergarten. How could she possibly make it on her own without my ever-present assistance? What would face my little girl as she walked out the front door?

From the shallow waters of her inexperience, the idea of school was an exciting adventure for my little Katie. From the depth of my understanding, the calm waters of her sheltered life were about to be blown fiercely by the storms of life I envisioned ahead. First, there was the school bus—a big yellow tanker of hazards (at least in my mind). The bus driver appeared like an apparition in my head. It only took a couple of minutes for me to conjure up a whole series of events leading to his arrest for reckless driving and drug dealing. The other children on the bus became a giant whirlwind in my mind. They swirled madly around a vortex of school-age frights, ready to pull in my little girl.

There might be a child on the bus whose character might turn out to be questionable. He might be innocently in love with my precious Katie now, but his intentions later on might be less than honorable.

There was also the possibility that Katie might get off the bus at the wrong school or the wrong bus stop. I could see her wandering around, afraid and crying, not knowing who to ask for help. Maybe I should ride with her this first time out. Even if she made it to school and somehow found her way to her classroom, how would she get along with her teacher? Katie could be headstrong and stubborn. I was convinced that the teacher would not know how to handle her.

My musings were interrupted by Katie, who said impatiently, "Mom, look at the numbers of the clock. You said that when it was 8-1-5, we should go to the bus stop." It was the moment I dreaded, 8 1 5. I gathered up Katie's brother and sister and put them into the double stroller for the trip to the end of the block where we would wait for the bus. Far too quickly, the school bus pulled up and stopped. I said goodbye to my small daughter with a reluctant kiss. I felt sure she would cry and refuse to get on the bus. She hugged me. Then, looking both ways before she crossed the street, she joined the line of children who waited to board the bus.

As Katie walked up the steps, I heard her say to the driver, "I am a kindergartner. Will you please make sure I get to the right place?"

The driver, a middle-aged man with a grandfatherly face, laughed and said, "Sure, honey. That's what I'm here for. My name is Mr. Bob. What's yours?"

"Katie."

"It's nice to meet you Katie," Mr. Bob said with a smile.

"Katie, come sit with me," I heard someone say as the driver shut the doors and the bus disappeared down the street, carrying away my daughter.

As I turned the stroller around and headed back to the house, I experienced my first flash of insight into a mother-daughter dynamic never addressed in my baby books. Until that moment, I hadn't understood that part of being a mother is learning to "let go" and have confidence in the child you've parented. With a pang of uncertainty, I realized that it was me who wasn't ready for kindergarten. Kindergarten is just a baby step in the long process of learning to "let go" I would face in the years ahead. After that morning, I found myself wondering what it was that I would not be ready for next.

Motherhood's tranquil and serene waters have been rippled many times over the years. Though I am better prepared for the idea that someday I will hand over the apron strings to her completely, I am still in no big hurry. I dawdled and daydreamed determinedly over my coffee the morning Katie took her driving test. I also find it necessary to remind my independent daughter, now a teenager, that she needs me whether she realizes it or not—even if it is just to give her money for the mall. Just about the time I think we have reached a new state of equilibrium in our relationship, she drops a new pebble into the pool.

But I have grown as a parent over the years. I am more objective about whether dangers are real or imagined. Letting go is Parenting 101, and I attended that class the day Katie went to kindergarten. ❧

Buckets of Buttons

GINNY HOBSON

Sometimes we as mothers learn life's lessons from our little girls.
Often it is in their childlike faith that the greatest lessons are learned.

When my daughter Jennifer was nine years old, she wanted a little yellow purse she had seen in a store. The purse cost $8.50. It was one of many colors on display, with four white buttons on each side to secure the fabric bag to a wooden handle. As our financial means were less than adequate, I tried to encourage her to save her money and hoped it would instill perseverance and diligence in her young spirit.

My own desire to persevere had long been dampened by a deluge of financial setbacks. An outpouring of problems that included cars in need of repair, replacing a washing machine, and average sales at my husband's business seemed to rain discouragement.

Several weeks went by. I had all but forgotten about the purse, but Jennifer had not. One morning she announced she had saved the money needed to buy her treasure from the department store. Astonished by her announcement, I cautioned her that the purse would probably be gone. Her little mouth began to quiver, but she said resolutely, "I know it's still there. I saved the money for the purse and prayed. Please, Mom, let's go and get it!"

We made the trip to the store. All the purses were gone from the display, but we spotted a lone yellow one on a clearance table. It was missing two buttons, shop worn, and on sale for $6. She was delighted, but I was less than enthusiastic. I knew it would be next to impossible to find two buttons that would fit and match the button holes to hold the bag together. Her sweet eyes sparkled and her long blonde hair bounced as she shook her head up and down to tell me that she was sure she could find buttons to fit. She would just pray again. How could this young little girl have such faith—so childlike yet so unconditional and so far from my own. Yet each mother yearns and hopes for her little girl's dreams to come true. So, we went home with a broken, slightly soiled bargain purse.

That night we searched through drawers and the button box to no avail. We called neighbors and friends. No one had the right kind of buttons. I began to doubt if we would find even a size match to hold the purse together.

Jennifer remained undaunted. She washed it tenderly and placed it by her bed with "special things" little girls put in their first purse.

The next morning my husband and I were awakened by our daughter's joyful cry, "Where did you find my buttons?" Sleepily, we replied, "What buttons?" She jumped up on our bed and opened her hand. Inside were two pearl white buttons exactly the same size and color of the other buttons. "They were lying on top of my purse when I woke up," she said triumphantly. There was not a doubt or question in her heart where they came from, only joy that they were there. She knew God had just known they were so very important to her.

Through Jennifer's eyes and faith, I learned something that day. Maybe it is the smallest of things that heaven notices and touches with a blessing to encourage our hearts. If God could answer Jennifer's prayer about missing buttons, perhaps He did hear my prayers and pleading for the downpour of mishaps to stop. I realized the buttons on the purse, though small, held it together, just like His love holds our lives together. If I would just believe, He would help me, too.

I decided I would trust Him. The sun *would* shine again. Since then I have received many "buttons." And my young daughter, who showed me how to have faith and believe, has through the years received bucketsful of "buttons" for her never-ending faith.

Seasons of the Heart

Blessed Is the Mother

SHERRY MORRIS

Blessed is the mother
whose tasks are a labor of love
For she is a willing servant
to her Heavenly Father above.

Blessed is the mother
who mends hearts and broken toys
For she shows her children kindness
and fills their lives with joy.

Blessed is the mother
who teaches her children to pray
For she gives them each a blessing
that remains throughout their days.

Blessed is the mother
who knows childhood years will pass
And spends the time she has for now
to make memories
that will last.

Spring is the season for planting the seeds of our relationship with our daughter. We begin as novice gardeners preparing the soil with a mixture of affection and instruction, tenderness with time-outs, love, and learning. Often with uncertainty, we sift through our own life experiences to try and find just the right mix of ingredients that will help these little seeds to grow. We anticipate anxiously the buds of companionship that begin to bloom.

Sometimes a gardener's greatest challenge is anticipating the weather. In the sometimes intense days of the next season of life, it is not easy to prepare for other influences that may affect the growth of our relationship. If we have prepared the soil carefully in the spring of our days together, our daughter's roots will likely stay in place and survive even if they do experience the elements. A pair of pruning shears and praying hands are the tools needed to survive this next season of the heart! ✂

Seasons of the Heart

Summer

*I will instruct thee and teach thee
in the way which thou shalt go.*

PSALM 32:8 KJV

A time to keep . . .
a time to build up

The more intense days of summer call us out to the porch where we can sit alone with our thoughts and sample the taste of sun-ripened fruit at the day's end. Like a parade in the hot July sun, memories float past, clear and sharp while we are living them, then hazy and dreamlike, as their impressions fade like the music of a band on a distant street. Never completely silenced, this band music—whether playing a discordant tune or a heart-lifting melody—lingers in our hearts and returns each time we find ourselves alone again, out on the porch, or sharing our thoughts as mothers and daughters.

The music of summer begins as daughters leave early childhood behind. A wise mother knows that throughout the next season of life she will need to balance nurturing with limits. Instead of bedtime stories and tucking her little girl in, she must set curfews and make rules. Instead of snuggling and rocking, she must insist that homework be completed before softball practice. Then, mother must face teaching her daughter the facts of life and how to drive a car. She has to become insistent about knowing who her daughter is with and where she is going and when she will be back. This season of life is much more demanding and holds more uncertainty for the relationship between mothers and daughters than the earlier, more carefree season of the heart.

Come sit in a rocker on the porch with us and visit these days. The fruit of summer is being served on these pages as slices of life. Some tart, some sweet, and some too hard to bite into. Each slice is a sample of a sun-dried taste of the past. Some of our tales are memories of scorching moments that leave parched, tender sensitivities. Some are stories that inspire glad tears. May each of us come out onto the porch, hear the music of the past, and taste again the flavor of nostalgia as summer's bounty is picked from the garden of life and shared.

A Note of Love

ROSALIND COOK

As soon as my daughter Amy could write, she began leaving notes for me. "I love you" written in a child's hand is a treasure that I cherish. Following her example, I began to write notes to Amy and her little brother. I would tuck them in their lunches or leave one on their pillow or stick one in a school book for them to find. Amy loved it. We often communicated through handwritten notes during her growing up years.

There is one note that I will keep forever. It reminds me of a very painful experience that happened when Amy was 12 years old. It represents to me the day my daughter understood that I was a fallible human being and accepted me for who I am.

Amy found a baby bird that had fallen from its nest. She called him Willie. Willie lived in a laundry basket on a heating pad in Amy's room and became a very important member of our family. On her own, Amy called a vet and found out how to care for Willie. Amy carefully fed him dog food on a toothpick almost hourly and gave him water from an eye dropper. It became apparent that Willie thought Amy was his mother.

Amy faithfully took her tiny charge out in the yard each day and let him hop around. Weeks went by, and the day came when his feathers were close to being "flyable." Amy asked me not to take him out while she was at school. I wasn't concerned that he was really ready to fly just yet.

One morning I took Willie outside with me thinking I would let him hop around while I worked in the yard. To my horror, Willie flew directly to the top of a huge pecan tree in our yard. I begged, pleaded, and cried hoping the little bird would come down from the tree. I even tried to tempt him with dog food. But it was no use. Willie flew from the tree and disappeared. With a pit in my stomach, I spent the rest of the day thinking about how I would tell Amy what had happened.

Amy cried all evening. When I tried to talk to her, she refused to speak to me. My words of apology seemed only to make her angrier. For two miserable days I got the silent treatment.

Finally, I sat down and wrote her a letter acknowledging that after all her diligent care and hard work, I had robbed her of an experience that should have been hers. I told her how ashamed I was of myself and how sad I was to have hurt her. I asked her to forgive me.

Later that day, after she had read my note, Amy left on her bike. She returned a little while later with two stuffed animals she had bought at a garage sale. She placed them on my bed with a note telling me I was forgiven and that she loved me very much. I cherish the note, and I keep the little stuffed animals in a drawer in my bedroom. They are markers of a time when my daughter understood for the first time that her mother has a few flaws in her character, but my daughter still found it in her heart to forgive. ☀

A mother strengthens you with her prayers, blesses you with her love, and encourages you with her hope.

Seasons of the Heart

But store up for yourselves treasures in heaven, where moth and rust do not destroy, and where thieves do not break in and steal. For where your treasure is, there your heart will be also.

MATTHEW 6:20-21

For Where Your Treasure Is

CARRIE BARNES

My parents built the home of their dreams. It was a lovely home, filled with the kinds of treasures that my father's success as a businessman brought to our family. Years of scrimping and saving and hard work had finally paid off. We were set to enjoy the fruit of our parents' labor. In the 1950s, among other things that made our house special was the addition of 100 percent wool carpet. Both of my parents insisted we take extra special care of our new home.

Then, a tragedy struck our family. My little sister, who was 11 at the time, became gravely ill. My mother moved 150 miles away to care for her in a hospital. She stayed for months during my sister's long illness and came home only briefly. Suddenly, my carefree life as a young teenager went from doing typical teenager school and church activities to managing a house for my father and younger brother. I had to cope the best I could. Overnight, I learned to cook and clean and take care of my 4-year-old brother. I missed my mother greatly during this time but knew that my sister needed her more.

Most of the time, I kept the drapes shut so I wouldn't have to dust often. I had also figured out that with the drapes shut it was hard to tell if I had vacuumed the corners of the room or not. But, the carpet that my parents were so proud of required care. The drapes needed to be opened each day to let in light. It was also supposed to be vacuumed regularly to keep moths from dining on the carpet fibers.

My little sister struggled to live. Just before her 12th birthday, she died with my mother and father at her side.

Grieving, my mother came home and once again took over as manager of our home. One day she was vacuuming the living room and discovered that there were moths feasting on her beautiful carpet. Tiny holes and bare patches laced the corners of the room. Knowing that it was my fault, my eyes filled with tears. As my mother turned to look at me, she said, "Moths in the carpet? So what? Carpet can be replaced. Precious lives cannot."

Not long after the carpet incident, I was practicing with my baton in the dining room. I accidentally broke the beautiful chandelier over the dining room table. Again, I waited for the reproach I knew I deserved. Mother only picked up the mess and said, "Light fixtures are temporary. People are forever."

My sister's untimely death was a tremendous loss to our family. But the lesson my mother learned through the experience was one she taught my brother and me. Losing my sister meant that one of mother's greatest treasures was already in heaven. She still encouraged us to take care of our home; but, she never again scolded us over trivial things. The change in her showed me that my brother and I were her only real treasures on earth.

My mother's change of heart also taught a deeper spiritual lesson. Our Heavenly Father has unconditional love for each of us. Whenever we mess up, we can hear Him up in heaven saying, "Moths in the carpet? That's nothing. Only My children really matter." This lesson is a treasure of the heart that will never be lost or destroyed, nor rust away. ☀

Girl Talk

JADINE NOLLAN

When I was young, my mom and I would engage in what we called "girl talk." These talks began in childhood but became more and more meaningful as I approached and moved into my teen years. During those years the definition of girl talk meant I did most of the talking (if not all of it), and my mom would listen patiently. She laughed when I laughed and seemed to enjoy the funny stories of the day's events as much as I did. She also listened intently when I was troubled or confused about a situation and carefully offered truthful and decisive advice. The more I listened to her and did the things she suggested, the more I trusted what she had to say.

When I began dating, there were countless girl talks about dating and boys. Mom would stay up when I went on a date to see that I made it home. She would lie across my bed at night listening and sharing until one of us would fall asleep. She respected and trusted me enough to give me the freedom to make my own decisions, but I learned that her experience was valuable in the lessons life was teaching me.

As the years have gone by, I continue to have girl talks with my mother. Now, I talk less and listen much more. I talk to my mom about motherhood and about my oldest daughter who is about to start her teen years. Mother's experience, understanding, and support are priceless to me as an adult. She's given me gifts that money can't buy and that I can never repay—the gift of time and the gift of love. She also taught me how to listen.

These are precious gifts I want to pass on to my children too, for these are the greatest gifts I believe any mother can give.

Without realizing it, my mother had begun a tradition, one that I will pass to my daughters and hopefully they'll pass on to their daughters. A tradition that ties our family generations together with love. The tradition of "girl talk."

Seasons of the Heart

The Vines in My Garden

SHERRY MORRIS

Sweet flowers on a tender vine,
Both needing love and care.
Two blossoms of a different kind
Each with love to share.

One is like a morning glory
Who wakes with the dawn's first light.
One is like a moon flower
Who thrives in a star kiss'd night.

If God made the morning glory
And the moon flower is His design,
He knows best how to care for His garden
And how to tend to His vines.

For daughters, like flowers, are different,
Enfolding and seeking God's plan.
Mothers, like gardeners, must prune them
And entrust them to God's loving hands.

I remember in the
solitude of a
moment shared,
my mother became
my friend.

My Daughter's 16th Birthday

GINNY HOBSON

My daughter Jennifer's 16th birthday was going to be just as I had imagined it would be—perfect. I'd arranged for a luncheon at a beautiful restaurant and invited four of her closest friends, my mother, and my three sisters. This time it was going to be done right. For it seemed no matter what I did as a mother I felt inadequate. I was always forgetting something. Monday, I forgot to tell her that her teacher called about an assignment. On Tuesday, I forgot to give her money for her school pictures. Thursday, I forgot her! I'd left her at cheerleading practice. Thank the Lord she would get her license soon!

I was busy trying to keep up with the schedules of my three children, work part-time, take care of the house and meals and somewhere in between be a wife. Mothers by profession are really jugglers trying to keep full plates on sticks spinning all the time. Occasionally and more often than not, they drop the plates. I was very good at that—the dropping part. I'd always have to call my mother or sisters to help me catch one.

This luncheon was going to be my make-it-up-to-you day, and I was anxious to show my daughter how much she was loved by her mom. Jennifer was so excited and looked beautiful in her 16th year of life. Truly, she was a gift from God to her dad and me. Even when I was amiss in my motherly duties, her disappointment would be reserved and most often she was understanding. This response made it harder for me to get upset with her for teenage infractions such as every morning using all the hot water. When she didn't meet my expectations, I would try to remind myself that I was always dropping those plates.

And alas, this morning was no different. Her room was a disaster to the second power and not only did she use up all the hot water, she took my shampoo out of my shower. As I was washing my hair with bar soap and getting madder by the minute, I realized I had forgotten the birthday cake. While admonishing my daughter, I told her to call her grandmother to pick her up so they could greet the guests since I had to retrieve the cake. She gave me the oh-no-not-again look and called my mom. I slid out the door and thought, "My mom's not going to believe this one," and then thought, "Oh , yes, she will."

By the time I found the bakery, paid for the cake, and started the 20-minute drive to the restaurant, I was berating myself. How could I have forgotten the cake? Even with my best efforts, I could not keep all the plates spinning.

I knew when I arrived at the luncheon I would see the disappointment in my daughter's eyes. My mom and sisters didn't even know the guests. I was supposed to welcome everyone, make suggestions on the menu, light the candles, and speak sweetly of what my daughter means to me. Instead I would be arriving 45 minutes late.

But when I arrived, I saw a most amazing sight. There was my daughter laughing, her eyes full of joy. She was graciously walking around the table telling each person how she appreciated each of them being there. My mother had thoughtfully seated each guest in between my sisters, and all were involved in fun teasing and reminiscing about their teenage years. Packages were opened, lunch had been served, and it was time for the cake. Instead of disappointment, my daughter greeted me with an excited, "Oh, my mom's here! Mom, this has been so much fun!" My mother patted my shoulder and brought me my lunch. My sister took the cake and cut it. Another sister brought us all in harmony with the "Happy Birthday" melody.

I looked around the room and suddenly realized that I wasn't really carrying all those plates by myself. My mother and sisters had always seemed to be there when I needed them to help with the balance. My "little girl" was so grateful for my love and was becoming a wonderful young woman. Ties of the heart and spirit had knit us all together for each other, and it was a strong and beautiful fabric. It was well-sewn and large enough for catching plates. The day of the luncheon was perfect and my plate was full of love!

A mother's

love is

like a rose

always

blooming,

forever caring,

always giving,

forever sharing.

My Mother and the Car

CARRIE BARNES

When I turned 16, my parents gave me a car. In my mind, a 15-year-old navy blue Dodge hardly qualified as transportation. To my parents, though, the car was adequate for my need to drive to school and church activities in the small town where we lived.

One day, I drove the "blue bomb" to school. On the way, the car began to sputter and spit just before it died and wouldn't go any farther. I was furious! Why did my mother send me off in a car that was almost as old as I was? Muttering to myself, I collected my books and belongings I needed for the day and started the long walk home. I stormed into the house and said with more than a trace of agitation in my voice, "That stupid old car just bit the dust. What are we going to do about it?" My mother didn't seem to appreciate the gravity of the situation. Since I was already late to school, she calmly told me that Dad would look at the car and she would take me to school. All day long I nursed the hope that the "blue bomb" had driven its last mile and that I would soon be the proud owner of a different—if not new—car.

After school was out, I caught a ride home with a friend. My mother was in the kitchen making dinner when I came in. "What's the bad news on my car?" I asked. My mother turned around smiling and laughed as she said, "Well, you know that cars do need gas to go."

I never got a new car, but I did learn to check the gas gauge.

From the Hands of an Artist

GLYNDA TURLEY

(AS TOLD TO SHERRY MORRIS AND GINNY HOBSON)

Glynda Turley's art graces the pages of this book.

Like a sketch begins to take shape in the hands of an artist, a mother takes the life of her child into her hands and paints traits of character, highlighting her child's gifts and abilities from the perspective of her own life experience. Whether she knows it or not, a mother is an artist. My mother, like her mother before her, did not think of her art of mothering as unique or special. But in my mind's eye, their art has remained in the foreground of my life, nurturing my gifts and abilities, and helping me see in clarity and detail how a mother's love is a masterpiece designed by her devoted heart and affectionate hands.

My mother was the opposite of me in appearance. She was tall and had beautiful hands with long slender fingers. Though she died when I was young, I can still close my eyes and see her loving hands doing many things: ironing my dad's clothing, icing a cake, dusting the furniture, sewing, comforting me, and folding in prayer. From her hands came hymns at the piano with words and music that echo in my mind still today. I was fortunate to have her guidance at the right time in my life. She taught me to follow my conscience as I made decisions. She also taught me to pray and trust in God.

My mother's art was to create loveliness when she had so little to work with in terms of material goods. She loved pretty things. She arranged and rearranged the furniture to keep things interesting. Her dressing table was always filled with beautiful empty perfume bottles and inexpensive costume jewelry, displayed just so. She was kind and beautiful and good, and the effect she had on the person I am is pressed deeply like a relief that has left a pattern of lovely memories on my heart.

44

Like my mother, my grandmother was an artist in her own way. In fact, if you can inherit creative genes, I'm sure I received mine from her. She could have been an artist if she had the opportunity. Instead she expressed her creativity through the clothing and craft items she designed, often from recycled garments, for family and friends. She gave these to anyone who entered her door. She would never have dreamed of selling anything she'd made.

My grandmother created beautiful gardens. These she nurtured with an artist's eye for color and texture. She tended her masterpieces of nature on either side of the porch while my grandfather sat and sang to me or read his Bible. She showed me how to take marriage seriously as she was truly a helpmate to him in every way as they ministered to others together. She cared for her own outward appearance but stressed inward beauty as being much more important. I can hear her saying, "Beauty is as beauty does." She encouraged busy hands on every day but the Lord's Day and used her Bible as a hands-on guide to daily living. Whether filling rows of shelves with colorful garden vegetables or sitting on the porch shelling beans, my grandmother's art of communicating the important things in life still rings true.

My mother and grandmother have been gone for a long time, and I miss them greatly. They didn't leave me money or worldly goods. They left me gifts of the heart much, much greater. They showed me life examples of being a Christian and left me great memories I will always treasure.

God has blessed my life richly with my own beautiful daughter Shannon. As my grandmother would say, "She's as beautiful inside as she is outside." Like her grandmother and great-grandmother before her, Shannon loves God and it shows. The art of mothering we learned from our mothers before us is one she is passing on to her children as well.

The hands of my mother and grandmother were the skilled hands of an artist each in her own way. The shades of their love colored my world with a legacy of character and wisdom. Though their lives were not highlighted by an artist's accolades, I thank God for these women in my life. For much of who I am and the good that I have done, I owe to them and their loving hands. ✺

Glynda Turley
©1995

Seasons of the Heart

As We Guide Our Children

SHERRY MORRIS

As we guide our children faithfully
along the path of life,
May we help them to find courage
as they're learning to take flight.

May we love them unconditionally
while we have them in our nest,
And guide them with the wisdom
that will help them be their best.

Then, as fledglings who are ready
to spread wings into the wind,
may we offer them our blessing
as a parent and a friend.

Many a delightful summer day is spent near the water, where the waves soothe us and surround us with a sense of timelessness. Cavorting like children through the inviting curls of water, we easily cast the cares of today out into the vastness. Prayer has healing qualities like the waves of the sea. Ever-washing and ever-changing the miles of shoreline within our lives, it can melt away past hurts and sorrows. If we allow God to work in our hearts, prayer's replenishing power cascades over the years and smoothes the edges of hard-heartedness. Prayer can also swallow up and wash away disappointments out into the vast sea of God's love.

Like the ocean ebbs and flows and skitters against the shoreline, mothers and daughters may come to the end of the summer in their lives and find themselves coming close to touching the grains of sand that have left an imprint of bitterness upon the shore. As the tide propels a wave of remorse forward, then just as quickly back again into the sea, the moment may pass and nothing is resolved. Again and again, mothers and daughters may come close to revealing the pain that hinders them from becoming as close as they could be.

The ability to forgive may not find its way onto the shore by nature's force alone. Sometimes, the restoration of the relationship comes through the celestial pull of a mother's or daughter's need to forgive or be forgiven. With words unspoken or only spoken through the power of prayer, kindred hearts can return to the time and place before summer's unforgiving rays robbed them of the joy of their relationship. For some, there is much to forgive. For others, it is just the residue of life that needs to be bathed in the fresh water of a new understanding and appreciation of being mother and daughter.

Autumn

Her children arise and call her blessed.

PROVERBS 31:28

A time to let go . . .
a time to mend

After the long days of summer, autumn is a season of change for mothers and daughters. Now a mother is faced with playing a supportive role while her daughter goes off to college, launches a career, and/or marries. When we who are daughters are young, it seems like forever before we leave home and go to college, get married, or otherwise go out to make our way in the world. At long last, our room at home becomes a storage place for left-behind childhood treasures. Autumn days are a time for preparing whatever life may bring.

As a mother stands at the door of a now empty room, the glowing light of autumn casts a golden hue on shadows of the past. In the gentle light of nostalgia, a mother recalls affectionately both the delightful mud pie days and the sometimes unnerving mayhem of life with her daughter. The room where her daughter grew up is now a place of quiet solitude for mother to dust as she fills the empty space in her heart with memories. Voices and sounds from the past—squabbles between her daughters, whispered secrets, and irrepressible giggles and tickling—add a kind of lonely melody to the pattern of days. The room that was thunderous with the noise of growing up is now silent. For a while, it may only be mom who remembers with pleasure the sounds of yesterday. She has lived long enough to appreciate the resonance of voices not always in harmony.

During the autumn years, a mother reaps a harvest that grew in both the sunshine and shadow of their days together. Standing by a window open to her future, a daughter gathers a lifetime of memories and stores them carefully in her heart. Like the barns of the harvest filled with nature's bounty, mothers and daughters fill their hearts with the kinds of memories that will nourish them through the brisk winds of change that blow throughout this season of the heart. ❦

Where's Mom Now That I Need Her?

JENNIFER HOBSON LAMB

The wedding was just wonderful,
So memorable and grand.
We hugged and cried as we said good-bye,
And I took my husband's hand.

But now the honeymoon is over,
And my own home beckons me.
Yes, marriage is quite incredible
As a member of a brand new team.

What a blessing to find true love
With this lifetime partner of mine.
But it seems one of his main concerns
Is that we eat on time!

And I guess his mom did not show him
Exactly what hangers are for.
It seems that his clothes just cannot find
Their way through the closet door.

Yes, my hubby is so wonderful.
He loves me—that I know.
But Monday nights I'll have to watch
Football—his most favorite show.

Well, I tried a little cooking;
I thought I was so prepared.
But words like braise and blanch
Gave me such a scare!

I unpacked all the wedding gifts.
I'm so thankful to our guests.
But a simple one-dish cookbook
Is the gift I like the best!

The housecleaning is so tiresome,
How do you clean bathroom tiles?
I've scrubbed and scoured, polished and shined
Until the glass reflects a smile.

Oh, the laundry seems to pile up,
I guess I must have forgot
That all items need to be sorted,
And colors can't be washed in hot!

I recently caught a cold
And wished for your chicken soup.
It warms the heart and the body,
Cures the chills or coughing croup.

I tried to plant some rosebushes,
I selected the perfect spot.
But after reading about the "pruning,"
I planted flowers in a pot!

I just can't believe how busy I am
With work and this home "stuff."
It seems the chores will never end.
How did you ever get caught up?

I'll have to learn all your tricks,
Those time-savers and shortcuts.
You'll answer all my pleas I know,
And wish me lots of luck.

In my younger days I never knew
Just how much effort it takes
To keep a household running smooth.
Mom, you never took a break!

Now I can see I'm not quite "too old"
To ask what Mom would do.
So, for the years gone past and the ones to come,
Mom—I'm so glad I have *YOU*!

Seasons of the Heart

51

Being confident of this,
that he who began a
good work in you will carry
it on to completion.

PHILIPPIANS 1:6

Glynda Turley © 1996

The Tools of the Sculptor

ROSALIND COOK
(As Told to Sherry Morris and Ginny Hobson)

If each of us is like a lump of clay molded and shaped by the experiences we have in life, then my mother used many different tools to sculpt me. When I was small, her words of encouragement helped me learn to walk and ride a bike. Her loving hands wiped away my tears when my knees were scraped in the process. As I grew older, my mother touched my life and molded my thinking by listening and offering guidance. Influences that might have kept me from reaching my full potential were chiseled away by her rules for proper behavior and her expectations that I would always try to do my best in all situations. Although my mother did not see into the future or know just who I would become, she had the vision of a sculptor to see the potential in my gifts and abilities. She simply nurtured the best way she knew how, using the tools she had, to release the person inside her small lump of clay.

Since I loved working with children, I chose a career as a special education teacher. I married the love of my life, Hal, and after the birth of our first child, decided to stay home. Although my days were busy, I found the time to begin sculpting figures of children. My mother was thrilled and always encouraged me. As I shaped and molded clay, I found I had a sculptor's vision to see and form representations of childlike faith and symbols of biblical truths. It soon became my passion. After a number of small successes led to some major recognition, I knew I had found my life's work and mission. Sculpting is a joy and a blessing in my life I love to share with others.

The morning of November 10, 1995, I attended the dedication of the most prestigious sculpture of my career. Somehow God had seen fit to bless me with the privilege to design and execute a monumental sculpture for the new headquarters of World Vision, the world's most extensive Christian relief and development agency. From the very beginning of this divine appointment, I saw the concept of Christ holding out the bread of life to the children of the world. This sculpture of Jesus with children coming to Him stands more than nine feet tall. My vision became a reality and was being dedicated to the glory of God.

My mother flew in to Seattle for the dedication. The evening before the event, she called me into her room and opened her jewelry box. She tenderly picked up a small, oblong rock and said, "When you were two years old you brought this rock into the house and exclaimed, 'Look Mom, it's Mary holding baby Jesus!' You saw in this rock something no one else could see. I have kept it all of these years knowing that God was going to do something very special with your life."

This little rock now sits in a glass dome in my studio. It is a reminder to me that the ability to sculpt is really not my ability at all. My hands are just the tools God uses to release the gift He gave me to bless and encourage others. My mother used the tools she had as a mother to release the gifts inside the child God gave her. With a sculptor's vision to see something beyond what was obvious, she trusted God to perform the work He began and believed that it was He who would bring His plan to completion in me.

I am now a mother of three wonderful children. The little rock my mother saved from the time I was a little girl is a reminder of my mother's vision for me, and that God, the Master Sculptor, often uses mothers to help mold His clay. ❦

A Mother's Prayer

GINNY HOBSON

I asked the Lord to bless you
as I prayed for you today,
To guide you and protect you
as you go along your way.

To add wisdom to your every step
to keep you in His care,
So just in case you stumble,
you'll know that He is there.

His love is always with you.
His promises are true,
And when we give Him all our cares
you know He will see us through.

So when the road you're traveling on
seems difficult at best,
Just remember I'm here praying
and God will do the rest.

Seasons of the Heart

A Different Kind of Mother and Daughter

SHERRY MORRIS

I remember the day my father remarried. The day of his wedding was also my 13th birthday. In my opinion, Daddy could have chosen another day to start a new life. After all, which was more important, his wedding or my birthday?

Not only was I annoyed with his choice of day for his wedding, I was less than pleased with his choice for a wife. Virginia was not my ideal candidate for the position. Why did he choose this woman who was so unlike anyone we had ever known? She was Catholic. We were Southern Baptists. She was a second generation Italian from Chicago. Daddy was from Oklahoma and was raised on a farm. Daddy was a quiet, gentle man and a homebody. Virginia liked to talk and laugh and spend time with friends. Daddy was a teetotaler. Virginia, horror of horrors, was known to have a glass of champagne at an anniversary party. Had my dad completely lost his senses? (I was still too young to realize that opposites attract.)

I distinctly remember feeling that it was my place to protect my father from this woman of the world. Not long after they were married we went to Chicago for Virginia's family reunion, and sure enough, she drank a glass of wine with her dinner. I promptly poured a soft drink for Daddy and announced to everyone at the table that my dad would have root beer.

Feeling intensely loyal to my mother, who had been gone since I was nine, my mind was closed to the very idea of having a stepmother, particularly one I would have to live with in the same house. Sharing my father with another woman and a couple of stepsisters wasn't a prospect I found appealing either. Cinderella and I would have something in common, I thought. I didn't relish the idea of my dad spending time with a woman who was not my mother.

As the months passed, I slowly began to notice that this woman had a few good points. Virginia was a great cook. After several years of my dad's cooking, I could really appreciate this quality. When I would let her, she would take me shopping. She helped me find clothes that were in fashion with the junior high crowd instead of the little girlish styles my dad would bring home for me to wear. This ability gave her a higher rating on my Stepmother Good Behavior Scale.

There were even some good things that came of having a woman in the house again. Virginia redecorated. Though Daddy had tried to create a home for us in the years before she came, he just did not have the knack for decorating. Faux black leather chairs and masculine accessories just did not create the cozy atmosphere I remembered from days gone by. Virginia's furniture, curtains, pillows, rugs, and other feminine touches transformed our house into a home.

Something unexpected and completely remarkable happened during the next two years. Although we experienced many of the troubles common to blended families, I began to feel a sense of belonging and connection. Four girls sharing a bathroom hardly encourages family unity. But having a stepsister who was old enough to drive became a definite advantage. I was willing to make concessions when necessary. Maybe I could open my heart to my new family, but I didn't know how to explain or share my thoughts. On my 15th

Seasons of the Heart

birthday and their second anniversary, I found a way to express what I felt about my home and new family. I wrote and sketched a book as a gift to Virginia entitled, "The House That Virginia Built."

In this book, written in pencil, I tried to describe how I felt about our home now that Virginia lived there. Room by room I drew the furniture, the walls, the pictures, plants, and even the cat. In rhymed verse, I described how the rooms of our home had changed since Virginia came to live with us. The kitchen was once a place where we ate Dad's burnt steak and watery instant potatoes. When Virginia came, the kitchen became a place for us to learn to cook simple recipes and bake cookies for our friends. It became a room where we gathered at the end of the day to set the table, fix a salad while she made dinner, and chat about our day.

The living room once was a room for watching television. When Virginia came, it became a place to sit in and visit with friends and family who came by for some of her great

desserts, coffee, and company. The bedroom used to be a place to sleep and get ready for school. When Virginia came, it became a place where we gathered at night in our pajamas to talk, do our homework, or make plans for parties and projects. The dining room was once a place where we piled our books after school. When Virginia came, it became a room where wonderful home-cooked meals were served on beautiful linens and china plates for a multitude of guests.

Though I don't remember all the pictures and verses that went into the book, I do remember drawing a picture of myself looking somewhat cross-eyed and the last line, "Most important is the love that Virginia built in her house so fine, and because of this we love her, and even her Catholic wine!"

Virginia cried and hugged me when I gave it to her. Though I still loved and cared deeply for my own mother, I had found a way to communicate my warmth and affection for this dear lady who became my daddy's wife. I think for both of us the book represented the day that we became more than just stepmother and stepdaughter. We became a different kind of mother and daughter, bonded by ties of genuine caring and love for one another. From then on, we have had a special tie to each other that has remained intact through many, many years.

I'm grateful that Virginia came to live at my house. I learned much from her about how to be a mother. She taught me that spending time together is a way to develop a relationship. Sharing chores or cooking can be the best time of day if it is a time when mother and daughter work together and tell each other about the day's events. Virginia demonstrated to me that mothering is creating the kind of home where children can have friends in and know they are welcomed. She showed me how to nurture as we talked in the car on the way to shop for clothes. Even when we experienced some of the storm clouds of being mother and daughter, she showed me that being a mother is a lifetime job. The ties that bind are not easily broken. Her willingness to invest time and love in me gave me many of the tools I needed to build love into the house for my family when I became a mother myself.

My disappointing birthday twenty-six years ago turned out to be a blessing. Dad gave me a gift that has lasted throughout the years. When I opened my heart to Virginia and her girls, I opened my life to new possibilities for love, friendship, and family ties. Today, my children call Virginia "Nana." Aunt Ginny and Aunt Cindy are very much a part of all our lives.

Though it's been redecorated and remodeled several times over the years, the house that Virginia built is still standing. Now its rooms are filled with wisdom and love for the next generation. ❦

Mother, My Friend

GINNY HOBSON AND TINA BENNETT

Mother, it is only now that I am older that I can truly see,

Just how much I've meant to you and how much you've meant to me.

You taught me how to love, to laugh, to work and play.

You taught me to trust God, and with you I learned to pray.

You taught me to believe in all my dreams and plans;

You taught how to build again when castles turned to sand.

You've always been my mother in whom I could depend,

And now I know that you've become to me, a cherished friend.

Mother, when I was young, your love was tender,
and though I'm grown, I still remember.

The Picture Gallery

JENNIFER HOBSON LAMB

It was 5:15 p.m. and the guests were due in less than two hours for my parents' 25th wedding anniversary party. The reception hall still wasn't ready. My dress arrived scorched by a friend who ironed it but was just trying to help. Even after months of planning, there were still a thousand details to attend to and dozens of people who needed my directions before my parents arrived.

"Surely it will all come together," I thought to myself as I pinned up more "memory" pictures of Mom and Dad on the photo wall. "I am taking two days off work after this," I told myself. I grabbed another picture to hang. It was a group photo of my mom, her sisters, my grandmother and me after my mom's graduation from nursing school. I had seen this photo a hundred times before, but as I pinned up a large color copy of it, the photo took me back to the reality of the moment it captured.

Mom had gone back to school part-time as a young mother and wife. As I searched my memory, I could recall her studying and going to class. She worked so hard and graduated with honors. Knowing what a hard time I had taking one graduate class while working, with no kids, I realized what level of time management she had to use to keep up those grades without sacrificing time with me.

I recalled many of our times together. There were summertime trips to the neighborhood pool, lemonade stands, holiday baking days, handmade Easter dresses and long-planned birthday parties. Mom strived so hard to make each season special and build a base of traditions that helped shape my personality and gave me stability and balance.

I remembered prayers at bedtime and playing our favorite butterfly game. Just like it was yesterday, I could see the joyful look on my mother's face as I burst out from under the covers, no longer a "caterpillar" but a big smiling "butterfly."

My mental trip to the past was interrupted as I saw the lights come crashing down from the decorative ivy tree. Thankfully, I saw my aunt scurry over to it and make the necessary adjustments. So I grabbed another photo to hang. This one was a picture of Mom and Dad in front of their first place of business. Once again, my mind began to wonder.

How could a psychology major and a nurse start a manufacturing business? So many people said the odds were against them. The demands on Mom's time became even greater as she helped my father build a business, worked part-time at the hospital, and now had two children to raise. But somehow there were still many special family routines that she made time for.

Whenever possible, she would pick me up from school. I wholeheartedly looked forward to the days when I would see her car enter the school yard. It just wasn't the same telling some relative or the carpool driver about my day. Mom's ears and heart always listened. We always had such a fun time talking. Whether it was figuring out a topic for a class project, counseling me on boys, or helping me figure out what to do with a sassy classmate, I always felt my needs were all she cared about during those car-ride conversations.

There were also the many times when she was the taxi-mom, toting a carful of kids over to our house for a sleepover. I also recalled Mom's incredible meals she served at dinner. A wife myself now, I know how hard it can be to get a home-cooked meal on the table after a busy day. But how vividly I could recall those precious times with all of us around the table, sharing stories of our days, and enjoying a delicious meal prepared by loving hands.

I remembered so many special events. Somehow, even with her busy schedule, Mom still made time to plan birthday parties, help me with homework, teach me how not to be afraid to catch the softball, make campaign posters with me when I ran for homeroom representative, and help me have a garage sale to pay for a spring break trip.

"Jennifer, do you realize people will be arriving in 20 minutes?" my grandmother warned me. Quickly, I began hanging more pictures and hoped none of my relatives could see my tears. Each photo was a reminder that we relied on each other through the years for fun, for support, and for love. "Tonight I'll hang some new photos in our family gallery," I thought to myself. "The snapshots will be of a daughter who understands a good childhood isn't measured by the number of ski trips or pairs of shoes you own. It's the love shown and the time invested by caring parents that make a portrait of a happy family."

My grandmother called, "Jennifer, they are here!" Someone snapped a photo of my mother's face. She was surprised and tears began to flow. Though it doesn't show in the photos taken of me that night, I knew that it was a different girl who smiled for the camera—a daughter who wanted to spend time showing her mother just how much she is loved. ❧

63

Seasons of the Heart

What Should a Mother Be?

CHARITY SELPH

Written to her mother Claudette for Charity's wedding shower.

A mother is many things. Someone who cares for her babies' needs, someone who holds her baby close at night rocking softly back and forth while singing precious lullabies. A mother has a special touch. Soft hands give you a feeling you remember. You felt it when she tended to your scratches and your cuts.

She is someone who always tries her very best to assure we grow up right. She makes sure we've said our bedtime prayers and are tucked in warmly at night. And if we ever awake during the dark hours of the night with cries of trouble or fright, she is right there to heal our hearts and dry our tears. She makes us eat our veggies and drink our milk, even when we say no. "These things will help you grow tall," she always said. Now I know.

A mother knows and takes into consideration being a teenager is a whole new exploration. Sometimes we are bitter and cruel and break the rules when the pressure of being a teen seems like too much. A mother is there to help you and give you her love, to expect you to give it your best at school and to abide by all those golden rules, make good grades so you can be someone important someday. And if a boy breaks your heart along the way, a mother is there to be at your side to hold you real tight and let you know everything is going to be all right.

A mother is there to clap and cheer as her grown-up baby holds her diploma near and leaves for college. A mother stands by her side and supports her efforts to gain more knowledge. A mother rejoices with her daughter the day the grown child says, "I Do," for the man she marries must be a very special person, too.

A mother knows it's time to let her baby go, build her own family and dreams, follow her own rainbow. But a mother is there to continue loving her daughter tenderly from her head to her toes, and on the day the now-grown woman packs her things to move away, a mother is there to say, "You know, sweetie, I have given you the wings to fly. And I know it is time for us to say good-bye. Just remember you will always be my baby girl to whom I sang precious lullabies."

That is what a mother should be. All this and more, Mom, you have been to me.

Seasons of the Heart

A Time to Weep . . .

SHERRY MORRIS

I sat at my desk buried in a stack of homework. The house was quiet. I was making great progress with my work when I heard sniffles coming from behind my mother's bedroom door. Opening the door, I found my mother reaching for a tissue to wipe her tears.

"Mom, what's the matter?" I asked.

"I'm just missing your sister," my mother replied in a trembling voice.

"Oh, Mom," I said quietly, as I sat beside her on the bed.

"I just can't believe she's gone," said my mother sadly, "I miss her so much. I keep hoping I'll wake up and find her snug in her bed. In the mornings, I expect to see her come flying down the stairs late to school. She was such a precious baby, and a joy to my heart." Tears filled her eyes again. "It just seems like the years have flown by. One day you have a little girl at your side and the next thing you know, she's gone. I have such wonderful memories of when you both were small. I wish I could turn back the clock to those days," she said wistfully.

"I miss her, too," I broke in, "but..."

My mother interrupted, "She was so willing to help out. She was so wonderful to run errands for me. I don't know what I'll do without her."

Finally, I could stand it no longer and burst out laughing. Mother looked bewildered. "She's not dead, you know," I said resoundingly, "she's just gone to college and will be home this weekend."

... Or a Time to Dance?

Having a daughter is a blessing and a joy. When a daughter leaves the nest, a mother sometimes has trouble filling the space left in her heart because her little girl no longer lives under her wing. Some people may respond by grieving the feelings of loss they may experience.

Others may recognize that they finally have fewer responsibilities and have time to think about their own goals and plans for the future. While watching daughters trying their wings, many women try on a few new wings of their own. Then each time their daughters return to the nest to visit, these mothers have new experiences and wisdom to share.

Is it "a time to weep" when the nest begins to empty? Or, is it, as the next verse in Ecclesiastes says, "a time to dance"? Maybe it is a little bit of both. If Mom can set aside her feeling of loss, she may find that now she has time to take dancing lessons. ❦

IN A LETTER TO HER MOTHER, LOUISA MAY ALCOTT WROTE . . .

"Whatever beauty or poetry is to be found in my little book is owing to your interest in and encouragement of all my efforts from the first to the last; and if ever I do anything to be proud of, my greatest happiness will be that I can thank you for that, as I may do for all the good there is in me."

As the golden hues of autumn begin to dim, the light of nostalgia acquires a new warmth that mothers and daughters share. As the blustery breezes of autumn winds give way to the stronger winds of winter, mothers and daughters feel the change in the air. As winter draws nearer, the joy of seeing the seeds sown, nurtured, and watered throughout their lives comes into full flower much like a poinsettia unfurls its beauty during the winter season.

Like all the seasons of life, winter has days of sunshine and shadow, fair winds and ill.

Both mothers and daughters prepare for this season by remembering that it is a time when kindred hearts must draw together for warmth and keep the fire on the hearth burning with a steady flame of caring and concern for one another. 🌱

Winter

He has made everything beautiful in its time.

ECCLESIASTES 3:11

A time to embrace . . .
a time for peace

Winter can be a season of serenity covered in a blanket of warm and loving reflections. When mothers and daughters draw close to the hearth of shared memories, the embers of the past cast a welcome light. As a daughter becomes a mother herself, she often has her mother close by for guidance and support. Her mother relives the joy of springtime in her life as she holds her grandchild close, snuggling once again into a rocking chair with a lullaby on her heart. The experience of motherhood becomes a common bond. During a season of the heart meant to be shared in front of a cozy hearth of mutual love and respect, mother and daughter often find a new depth to their understanding of one another.

For mother, now a grandmother, winter's joy can be chilled by sorrow. The sorrow of losing her own mother may become one of life's most deeply felt tragedies. Like an angel in the snow, the impression of mother's life melts away slowly; but her mother's memory remains indelibly imprinted into her heart.

With a tea kettle on the hearth and a coverlet of wisdom over her shoulders, mother settles into this season of the heart. She is ready to sit in a rocking chair long enough to read stories to her grandchildren. Though her days may be filled with a job or other responsibilities, this is the time in her life when she reflects back and remembers where she came from. As she wonders about the people of her past, she may begin to look for clues about them. Her mother's tea set becomes a family treasure. Her grandmother's sewing chest comes into the living room as a prominent display. Mother begins to connect the past with the present and finds ways to preserve tradition and family history into a legacy of the heart.

The coziness of time spent together and the shared history of mothers and daughters kindle embers of the past in their hearts. Sitting beside these embers, they may remember how the flame in their relationship blazed, then faltered, and began glowing again as they lay the kindling of the past into the fire. Not all shared memories between mothers and daughters are happy ones; but, the season of winter has a way of bringing these kindred hearts together once again to bask in the comfort of a warmth that emanates from this unique relationship. ✳

The Heritage

GINNY HOBSON

Many times in life we are able to step into and live for a brief moment in the past. These special moments come as mothers and grandmothers weave for their children stories from the fabric of yesteryear. Like quilt pieces snipped from the fabric of time, each of us must stitch these memories into a legacy. Because memories are gathered over the years, each of us who stops to listen finds we have pieced together a legacy of the heart to share with the next generation.

My husband was in the Navy when we married and Grandmother Spatafora came to my wedding. "Nana" was a very kind, robust woman of much quiet wisdom and great love for all her 10 children and 24 grandchildren. I had never spent much time with Nana, as she lived 700 hundred miles away. We occasionally travelled to see her, but our visits were short and combined with bustling cousins, aunts, and uncles. Her Italian cooking was sought after, and family times meant food, noise, and laughter.

It was the first visit to our home she had made, and I was moving away the very same week. A few days after the wedding, my husband returned to his assignment, and I was left to gather and box our wedding gifts and join him in a week.

With my mother and dad at work and my sister at school, my nana and I were alone for several days. She lovingly wrapped and sealed boxes for hours as we packed all my belongings of two decades. My heart was joyful to start a new life with the man I loved, yet my heart was saddened to leave those I loved the most. How could I not be close to my mom whom I called for any such thing, who made me my favorite desserts and had been there every time I needed her for my whole life? Tears filled my eyes one afternoon and I began to cry softly as my nana was tying the last box.

"It's alright to cry! I know," she said. "I had to leave my mama." How did she know what I was thinking? There had been so much excitement and happiness for days, but it just seemed like a flood of sorrow swallowed me up in a great gulf of homesickness.

She held me for one moment and then gently began speaking of days, years, and generations gone by. Her story revealed a wonderful loving mother who decades before had taught my nana how to cook and clean, laugh and love, and brighten each of her children's lives with the light of her love. This woman had lived thousands of miles away, and my own grandmother had cried and said goodbye to her 72 years ago. She never saw her again. I listened as she wove a beautiful tapestry of memories in my soul, memories I would allow to wrap warmly around my heart whenever I needed their family warmth.

Her glistening eyes and smiles much younger than her age brought to life my great-grandmother's life and days. Gardens and flowers grown for times together that cultivated and bloomed our family love. "You always take your family with you," she said and then told me of the day she left her mother and father.

She boarded a ship for America some 3000 miles away to meet my grandfather, who had gone before her and worked to send her passage. She described her journey of three months in steerage, the hardships she had faced, the deaths of children on board, and the deep concern she had for her own tiny daughter she had brought with her. She seamed together the years of coming to a strange country with a new language and the birth of my mother. She opened up the years of my heritage and showed me that strength, courage, and perseverance were part of my own fabric. I was knit together with these very threads of character she was now sewing in my mind. They were becoming permanent designs in the fabric of my life.

She then described my own mother's journey here during World War II. She described how my mother cried and didn't want to leave her parents, sisters, and brother. "And I told your mother and I tell you, too," she said. "This you have to do," she knowingly and simply stated. "You go and be with your husband. God—He will go with you."

And 30 years later she was so right. I wanted to hug and love the beautiful young woman that she once was who had gone through so much and set our family course with such strength. So I held tight to my nana who had given me one of my most cherished gifts I would treasure forever—a heritage of memories.

Starting a home and family far away from your roots intensifies the love you have for your own children and those far away. Though you are separated by miles, your love is not. The heritage remains and covers you with its endearing embrace for all your years to come. ✳

Seasons of the Heart

That's What Little Girls Are Made Of

SHERRY MORRIS

When I was a little girl, I loved to go to my grammy's house. It was a place of wonder, filled with lace doilies and windup clocks, shelves of books and old photographs, a foot-pedaled pump organ, and most marvelous of all, antique dolls. Grammy's collection included dolls with china heads, dolls with painted porcelain faces, and dolls whose "kidskin" faces were crackled with age. Some were dressed in taffeta and lace, and some were so delicate and beautiful they were just to look at.

Grammy's special dolls were displayed on a four-post bed in her guest room. I would stand at the foot of the bed and gaze at her dolls, wanting to touch them. I had to be content with looking, though their dresses were made of lace and ribbons, and they beckoned me with their eyes and beautiful hair. Whenever I spent the night, Grammy would turn down the covers on the four-post bed for me to dream in, after she had carefully placed the dolls on the mahogany dresser. I would snuggle under the thick comforter and stare at the dolls in the little bit of light, left on so I wouldn't be afraid. I knew that as soon as I closed my eyes, the dolls would begin to dance and have magical adventures while I slept. Try as I might to stay awake, the dolls had their wonderful escapades without me watching. I know because I saw all the fun in my dreams.

Grammy kept a special box of dolls tucked away in a closet that were just meant for little girls to play with and dress up. She told me that the dolls belonged to my mother when she was a little girl. I spent many happy hours dressing my mother's dolls in tiny clothes and shoes. It was hard for me to imagine my mother as a little girl playing with Grammy's dolls. Grammy said my mother had dark curly hair like mine. I knew how to take care of mother's dolls because I knew how she took care of me. I served the dolls tea in little china cups and saucers. I read stories to the baby dolls. I sang lullabies to them, bandaged their boo-boos, and kissed away their tears.

When I was older, I asked Grammy why she liked to collect dolls. She told me when she was a little girl all she had was one rag doll. She dearly loved her doll and played with her until the doll fell apart. Grammy never had another one. She made sure her own little girl had several dolls to call her own. After my mother grew up, she and Grammy enjoyed shopping for dolls, finding them in antique stores, garage sales, and flea markets. Each trip to search for treasures became a special memory. Some dolls caught their eyes because of some unique detail. But more often, she and my mother brought home a doll just because it had captured their hearts.

My grandmother's love for dolls is a legacy she passed on to me that I am sharing with my daughters. Thank heaven for little girls. I would be embarrassed to have collected a houseful by myself! Just as I grew up learning how to be gentle and loving to my babies when I played with dolls, my little girls have grown up bandaging their dolls' boo-boo's and kissing away their tears. Some of the dolls in my daughters' room are just to play with and enjoy. Others are ones that my girls tell their friends to look at, but don't touch, because they are special. Like their mother and grandmother before them, my girls have learned the fun of shopping and finding dolls to cherish and display. The love of dolls we share is a legacy they will pass on to their own daughters.

Someday I hope to be a grandmother. I want to have a place of wonder, filled with lace doilies and windup clocks, shelves of books and old photographs, and my most wonderful collection of dolls. In my guest bedroom, there will be a four-post bed and a comforter for my precious granddaughter so she can dream. In a closet, I will have tucked a box of dolls and clothes for her to make some memories of her own. And if she ever asks me why I treasure my dolls, I will tell her that in every little girl's heart are dreams about growing up, doing wonderful things, and having all kinds of exciting adventures. Just as my grandmother showed me that dolls help little girls to dream, I want her to know that dolls and dreams are lovely things, and that's what little girls are made of. ✳

My Mother's Chicken Soup

GINNY HOBSON

My mother's remedy for any illness my sisters and I had as little girls was a bowl of chicken soup. She would bring it piping hot on a tray and we would sip its wonderful flavor and feel warm inside. She said it would cure anything. Though it was many years before medical research confirmed the healing attributes of chicken soup, my sisters and I believed her. After all, we always got better.

Her other prescription for our maladies was not as endearing—a bath. She always made us take a bath. Fever, coughing, spots or not, into the tub we would go dragging our blankets behind us. We moaned and pled, "Mom, I'm too tired," or "Mom, I'm sick!" But we were still soaked in a hot tub with the promise that afterward we would feel much better. After the hot soak, steam, and scrubbing of skin, we usually discovered that she was right. We did feel better. How did she know?

From generation to generation, the practical how-to's of mothering skills are passed down. My mother knew the healing properties of chicken soup and the miraculous healing properties of bathing because her mother had taught her. As a young mother with children of my own, I prescribed the same treatments. Bowls of hot soup and tub baths over objections and whining were always my own "mother's orders."

Then the day came when this motherly prescription came full circle. My patient was my mother. She became seriously ill with pancreatitis. My sisters or I stayed around the clock with her at the hospital. She was very weak and in a great deal of pain, only able to take liquids. For the first time in my life, I saw my mother's frailty and realized what a loving, generous, and wise woman she was.

All my teenage years of indifference, arguing, and anger melted before my eyes and only the good in every year remained. She could speak only in broken sentences in

between fitful sleep mixed with pain and feverish hallucinations. With each passing hour I realized more and more how much I needed this woman to teach me and help me raise my children and to guide me in my marriage. "Mom," I would say every day, "you just have to get better."

On the third day, my motherly genes engaged and I become the mom. Though I'd hoped it would never happen, it was as though our roles reversed. So I determinedly ordered chicken soup from the kitchen. My prescription for her was chicken soup for breakfast, chicken soup for lunch, and chicken soup for dinner. I spoon-fed her like she was a child. She smiled weakly and said it did taste good. Then I filled the tub. She had been awake with no fever for an hour, and I felt now was the time. Of course she did just what I expected her to do. She moaned and pleaded and begged saying, "I am too sick for a bath."

But I was undaunted by her pleas. Just as she was undaunted by my pleas and just as her mother was undaunted by her pleas when she was a child. "Come on, Mom," I said briskly. "You know you will feel better."

She was so weak I had to bathe her completely myself. While I worked, I imagined all the care she had given me when I was a little girl. And I knew how much I really loved her, because of and in spite of all we had been through together.

She sighed in relief as I washed her back and smiled when I tickled her toes. Bubbles and powder completed the loving massage I gave her. Weakly and gently, she returned to her bed and simply said, "I do feel better. Thank you, honey."

Her eyes began to twinkle as she ate another bowl of chicken soup I placed before her. The doctor came in and stood in awe. "Well, well," he said, "I just received the lab report on you. You do not look at all like the patient described in this report." My mother and I looked at him in surprise. I quickly took him aside and asked him what he meant. He responded tenderly, "Her lab reports indicate that she should be in a coma by now."

In that moment, I felt terrible. I had made my poor, sick mother take a bath and risked her fragile health! She had tried to tell me how sick she was, but to no avail. I dared not tell the doctor what I had done. He asked me, "So what have you two been doing here that she looks so wonderful?"

My mother replied, "I feel better, too. My daughter made take me a bath." Ugh! It was out. My sin was confessed. "And I have eaten this wonderful chicken soup."

"Well," he smiled, "medical science does not always align with a patient's prognosis. Whatever you are doing, keep doing it."

A rush of relief spread over me as I smiled weakly at my mom. The doctor added as he left. "I am amazed at her. She looks much better."

In three weeks, she was out the hospital and eating her own chicken soup at home. Our family thanked God that she had recovered completely.

In our family, chicken soup is a heritage, and a bath when you are sick is a birthright. It goes right along with the love, character, and strength in the legacy a mother passes on to her daughters and becomes even stronger when the daughter becomes the mother. ✳

To My Mother

GINNY HOBSON

When I was just a little child
you were always there for me.
You'd pick me up and dust me off
and mend my scraped-up knees.

You've taught me that love and family
are the things that mean the most,
and through the challenges of life
you've kept this family close.

You've given so much of yourself
in everything you do
but now that I'm grown up,
please know
that I'll be here for you.

A Time to Forgive

SHERRY MORRIS

The new pastor shook my hand warmly and smiled. "Sherry," he said, "please remember that I am here to talk to if you need me." I looked at him in surprise. How did he know about what was going on in my life?

I liked our new pastor very much. He was a young man with energy and enthusiasm that was contagious. Here he was offering a hand of friendship, and probably some pastoral counseling, though I wasn't sure I wanted to talk to him.

His words had warmth and sincerity in them. To my surprise, I responded positively and said I would call for an appointment later in the week. I scheduled the appointment and spent the week before in turmoil with my own thoughts. How could I tell Mike about a whole lifetime of anger toward my mother?

The day she didn't come home was etched in my heart with crystal clarity. Even though I had never heard my parents fight or even say a cross word to each other, for days before she left I sensed that something was wrong. Afternoons suddenly seemed long until she came home from work in the evenings. Even while I played in the shade of the mimosa trees in my grammy's yard with my friends, I listened anxiously for her car. Then, the day came when the car did not turn in the driveway.

Grammy seemed concerned when she called my dad to tell him that Mama had not picked up my little sister or me. Daddy apparently asked her if we could spend the night. All evening long I listened for the phone.

The next evening, Daddy came to pick up my sister and me. He told us that our mother didn't want to live with us anymore. He said she would be living somewhere else and that we would get to see her sometimes. I could hardly breathe while he talked. Anger, confusion, and a sense of hopelessness overcame me that stayed with me all of my life. Even now, as a young married woman, I struggled to keep those same angry feelings away.

Though I didn't live with my mother from that day on, I did visit her house on weekends. She said she loved me. In fact, she repeated the words over and over to me. Although I tried to accept what she had done, the feelings of abandonment were sometimes overwhelming. I could never once remember her saying she loved me before she left home. Somehow her words didn't add up to what she had done.

Eventually, my mother remarried and then divorced again. Her life spiraled downward around a vortex of prescription medications and tranquilizers until she finally ended up on the psychiatric floor of a hospital. After treatment, she started coming to my church. I was less than pleased with this arrangement. It seemed hypocritical to me that I was supposed to act like her loving daughter when my feelings about her were less than amiable. Then, my new pastor came to our church. I didn't think anyone at church knew me well enough to have guessed that I felt hostility toward my mother. I felt fairly sure I had at least appeared in control when she was around.

I arrived on time for my appointment with Mike. He welcomed me into his office and said, "Sherry, I have to tell you that God laid it on my heart to pray for you and ask you to come and talk to me."

I wish I could describe what I felt in that moment. Mike didn't know about my relationship with my mother, but it seemed possible that God did. I may have hidden my feelings from my fellow church members, but I couldn't hide my feelings from Him. I knew it was no accident I was in Mike's office that afternoon. I was ready to let go of a burden that had weighed me down most of my life. My heart began to spill over as I talked about my mother. Every grievous thought I had over the years reared its ugly head and burst from my mouth in an angry tirade of words and tears. The more I heard myself talk, the more I realized that I was also angry with God. How could He have allowed my mother to abandon me?

I remember Mike listening patiently. I do not remember what he said to me that day, but I do know we prayed and asked God to take away the hurt and anger in my life, and to help me forgive my mother. When I left Mike's office that afternoon, I left behind a burden that had held my heart captive for more years than I wanted to admit.

I am thankful God sent Mike at a time when I was ready to listen. My mother soon began to genuinely turn her life around. She became active in another church and became a tremendous support to my younger sister Cindy. Eventually, a healing of our hearts took place that resulted in a new, loving relationship between my mother and me.

Almost five years later, I got a call that changed my life again. Mama had spent the evening baby-sitting my sister's two children. She had just finished making a new, meticulously detailed outfit for my brother's little girl and laid it across the sewing machine. Then she died suddenly of a heart attack as she sat in her living room. She was only 48.

It seemed unfair to me that my mother was taken so soon after she had been restored to me. But I also knew that I could not sow more seeds of bitterness and unforgiveness into my life. My mother once again was no longer a part of my day-to-day experiences, but the memories we shared for the last five years of her life were good ones. Though it is still disquieting to reflect back to the many difficult years in our relationship, I know that even those years helped to form my ability to mother my girls. For the lessons I learned from my mother about what not to do are as valuable as the lessons I learned about what to do right.

If I had found it in my heart to forgive her sooner, would we have had more good years together? I will never know. I only know that the lesson I carry in my heart is that now is the time to forgive. ❋

Mom, you once held my hand.
You'll always hold my heart.

83

A Message for My Mother

SHERRY MORRIS

There is a love I feel this year as I think about the days

When messages are often sent to loved ones far away.

It's a love that once was given, but now the giver's gone.

The love that came from Mother within me still is strong.

Though my feelings need expression, my heart is overflowing.

I have a calm assurance from the certainty of knowing

That I possess a messenger who intercedes on my behalf.

The promise of the scriptures say all I need do is ask.

So Heavenly Father will You send for me

A message to my mother?

I know she's there at home with You.

Please tell her that I love her.

Becoming a Grandmother

GINNY HOBSON

When my daughter and son-in-law asked me to be present at my first grandchild's birth, I felt it was a special blessing. I awaited anxiously the day of this soon-to-be miracle so I could share in this lifetime event.

At my own daughter's birth, my mother had been five hundred miles away. I had not experienced the joy of having her close by when I held my first child. Even though she could not be with me, my mom was always there for me. She shared in both the joys and the difficulties of being a new mom. In phone calls, cards, and prayers, she lifted me up with words of encouragement and understanding. When Jennifer cried with colic for three nights straight, my mother talked to me for an hour on the phone and let me cry. A letter from her made ordinary days seem special and somehow, though far apart, we were always connected by our love for each other.

One sparkling June afternoon, my daughter Jennifer gave birth to a beautiful baby boy. Chandler came tender and wide-eyed into the world. I lovingly kissed my daughter and her husband and we all cried. David my son-in-law gave me the honor of cutting the cord of my new grandchild. What joy! As I cut the cord, Chandler became his own person. He was not physically attached to his mother anymore. This precious baby had a new connection to his mother and father, an even stronger attachment of the heart.

As I held Chandler in my arms for the first time, I realized that his mother, Jennifer, would need me now in a different way than she had in the past. Our relationship was on new ground. It was rich with an even greater love than we had known before. For as they gave me this precious one so fresh from heaven, I felt a love so strong that it transcended generations. I saw in him my mother's skin color, so like my own. I saw my dark hair and my husband's round chin. I kissed each hand and held each foot and remembered 26 years ago the joy I felt the day they gave me Chandler's mother for my own. I felt blessed to live so close to my daughter and experience this new gift of life. I also knew the time had come to loosen the ties of my own heart to my child and let her begin to sew together heartstrings for her new family.

As attachments of the heart connect one generation to the next, I had learned the art of being a grandmother from my own mother. When I heard Chandler's first sweet cry, I felt our family's heartstrings extend another generation. I would strengthen David and Jennifer with love, prayers, and support should their ties become unraveled, and be there for them, just as my mother had been there for me. ✳

Mother, the cherished heirlooms that we hold dear are the treasured memories of your love through the years.

Our Family

GINNY HOBSON

Our family is a circle
without beginning or an end,
Always bending, never breaking,
in this love we can depend.

Love holds us all together
as in life we travel round,
From one generation to another
years of love are handed down.

When crisis comes upon us
and pulls us end to end,
If God is in our center
we know that we will mend.

So, remember in this family
you are a special part
Of a love that starts with God
and lives within our hearts.

One More Thing for Mama

Perhaps it is just the nature of our finite thinking that erroneously compels us to believe death ends a relationship between mother and daughter. Though the mother's ability to be influenced by her children ends with her death, her ability to influence her daughter's life continues long after she is gone. A daughter remembers many things about her mother. Memories of her favorite sayings, her hobbies, her counsel and guidance, and even her quirks and idiosyncrasies form a sense of connection that stays with a daughter for the rest of her life.

Speaking as a daughter who has lost her mother, I still look for ways to connect with her memory. As the years have passed and my memories grow dimmer, I long to find a part of her within me—something I have missed and did not know was there. I repeat her favorite idioms to my children, "You won't understand until you have children of your own," and "Because I said so."

For a time right after she died, I took up sewing because I felt closer to her as I worked with the patterns and cloth just as she did when I was a little girl. My children even say that like my mother, I've been known to walk around muttering to myself when I'm frustrated or just have too much to do.

Though I still feel a sense of connection to my mother, I feel a sense of loss in my life on holidays and other times that were meant to be shared with her. No longer do I buy a Mother's Day card or a Christmas gift for her. Instead, I buy a flower arrangement and place it on her grave twice a year. Even as I lay down the wreath, I know that I do it for myself, to bring a small measure of comfort. My mother does not know that I picked the lilac one because it was her favorite color. Since she died before I had a chance to say good-bye, I have always felt that I wanted to tell her I loved her, to do one more thing to show her I cared. It took another funeral to help me realize there is still something I can do to honor my mother's memory in a way that would please her greatly.

"Sherry, it's your Aunt Carolyn on the phone. She's on line 6."

Seasons of the Heart

"Thanks." I was buried in paperwork and glad for the interruption.

"Hello."

"Are you busy?" Carolyn asked.

"Always, but what's up?" I replied.

"I just called to tell you that Uncle Charlie passed away," Carolyn said sadly.

"I'm sorry to hear that. Let me think," I said with a bit of hesitation in my voice, "Uncle Charlie was Aunt Iza's husband, right?"

Carolyn answered patiently, "Yes, Iza is your grandpa's sister. The funeral will be this Thursday at 2:00. The church is serving dinner for the family at noon."

"Let me check my calendar," I said quickly, "I think I can come for the funeral."

"What about the dinner?" Carolyn said with a trace of impatience in her voice.

I have to admit the question took me by surprise. Yes, I knew that technically I am family. But I barely knew any of that branch of the family.

"Well . . ." I hesitated, "I have a feeling that I'll barely make it to the funeral Thursday. I don't think dinner is a possibility."

Aunt Carolyn sounded disappointed as she said good-bye. Her reaction puzzled me. "Why would it matter if I was at the dinner or not?" I thought to myself. "Most of the people there I haven't seen but once or twice since I was a child." I really hated to give up an afternoon I needed for work to go to a drawn-out funeral with people associated with events and places largely unfamiliar to me.

Thursday came. My sister and I arrived a little early at the church and joined the family in the dining area. Aunt Carolyn and my mother's other sisters greeted us with smiles and hugs. As we made the rounds of the room, we were introduced, in spite of the fact that both my sister and I are both nearly 40 years old, as "Marilyn's girls," to circles of timeworn faces. Heads nodded and eyes brightened as my mother's kin greeted us warmly.

"I'm your mother's cousin. Did she tell you about the time . . ." said one.

"I remember when your mother . . ." said another.

"I bet your mother never told you . . ." said yet another.

As we made the rounds of the room, my sister and I learned a great deal about our mother from people who knew her in times and places distant from our memories.

After only a few minutes of hearing tales from these distant relatives, I began to understand why it was so important to Aunt Carolyn for my sister and me to come to a funeral of a relative we barely knew. Just in being there, my sister and I had helped to complete a piece of a family circle that had been lost many years before. If for no other reason, we were there to represent our mother whose absence was still strongly felt by her kin, especially her sisters. It was comforting to know that the mention of her name even years after she was gone still brought a smile to the faces of those who knew and loved her.

I no longer dread funerals or gatherings of distant relatives. I know now that I have a place at the church with the family, regardless of how obscure or removed my relationship might seem. Even years after her death, I am still my mother's daughter, still representing in the eyes and hearts of her family the memory and legacy of Marilyn.

It's nice to know there is still one more thing I can do for Mama. ✳

The journey through the seasons is different for each of us as women, yet each of us shares the journey. Although mothers and daughters see the journey from unique vantage points, we are each passing through the circle of life. Sometimes it is just the difficulty of seeing life from the vantage point of the other that causes strain between us. Through the passage of time and the seasons, each has a greater potential for understanding the other's season of life. From the first hint of spring to the last spark in the fire on the hearth of winter, mothers and daughters influence one another's thoughts, emotions, decisions, and ways of relating to each other.

In remembering the seasons of the heart, each of us can recall the good times and the bad we experience as a mother or daughter. The writer of Ecclesiastes teaches us that there is a season for everything and a time for every purpose under heaven. Yet we may find it difficult to fathom the big picture and fully appreciate that we are just traveling through the seasons. Good and bad times are a part of the same big picture. Against the backdrop of the seasons, the good times and bad times are just different shades of the same experience. Maybe the secret of getting through some of the more tumultuous days is just to remember that God makes all things beautiful in His time.

Whether the memories that mark the seasons of your heart are fresh with the newness of living or weathered by the passing of days, we hope you have found a sense of connection to your own mother or daughter on the journey with us through the pages of *Seasons of the Heart*. Understanding the past, celebrating the present, and looking forward to a future together through the eyes of love bring us each a little closer if we are willing to share the seasons of our hearts. ✳

A Memory of My Own

Author Biographies

GINNY HOBSON lives in Sand Springs, Oklahoma, with her husband, Dan, and sons, Daniel and Jordan. Ginny's daughter, Jennifer, and son-in-law, David, recently gave Ginny and Dan their first grandchild, Joshua Chandler. Ginny and Dan work together at their company, The Carpentree, which produces framed art with inspirational verse and scripture.

SHERRY MORRIS also lives in Sand Springs, Oklahoma, with her husband, Steve, two daughters, Katie and Kelly, and a son, Adam. She is the children's minister at Angus Acres Baptist Church where she works with lots of mothers and daughters.

Sherry and Ginny became sisters in 1971 when Ginny's mother, Virginia, married Sherry's father, Don. They became a family with four daughters and one son. Many of the memories they share come from their days together in the same family and from their experiences with daughters of their own. Both agree that being a daughter is much easier than having one. They also agree that having a daughter is like "growing" your own best friend.

94

GLYNDA TURLEY is a renowned artist in America, well-known for her romantic landscapes and florals that recall simpler times. According to Glynda, her greatest accomplishments are her children, Shannon and Shon, and four grandchildren. She and her husband, Jerry, live in Heber Springs, Arkansas. Her art graces the pages of this book.

OTHER CONTRIBUTORS (in alphabetical order):

CARRIE BARNES (Tulsa, Oklahoma) and her husband, Jerry, have one son, Chris, and one daughter, Mary. She worked with preschoolers for many years as a speech teacher and is now an art designer for The Carpentree. With wisdom and concern, she lovingly "mothers" all of those she spends her days with there.

ROSALIND COOK (Tulsa, Oklahoma) is a nationally recognized sculptor. Many of her creations embody a sense of childlike faith that endear her works to her many fans and collectors. Rosalind is the mother of a daughter, Amy, and two sons, Mark and Clint. She and her husband, Hal, share a home and studio in Tulsa.

JENNIFER HOBSON LAMB (Tulsa, Oklahoma) is Ginny's daughter. Jennifer is a CPA and has an MBA, but recently with the birth of her first child, Joshua Chandler, she received her most sought-after title: MOM. She works part-time for her parents' framed art company, The Carpentree.

MARTHA MEEKS (Sand Springs, Oklahoma) is the mother of three boys, Ben, Sam, and Chris, and the mother of one daughter, Amy. She is the wife of Scott Meeks, Minister of Music at Angus Acres Baptist Church. She and Scott are originally from Houston, Texas, and have ministered at Angus Acres since 1989.

JADINE NOLLAN (Sand Springs, Oklahoma) grew up in a home with three sisters. With two daughters and one son of her own, she spends her days teaching daughters from age 5 to 18 how to jump up and down and yell. She's taught cheerleading for more than 10 years.

CHARITY SELPH (Tulsa, Oklahoma) is the daughter of John and Claudette Selph. Charity's mom, Claudette, is the director of the Parent Child Center of Tulsa, a nonprofit agency dedicated to helping families develop healthy relationships with their children. Charity is a play therapist for the agency.

SUE RHODES SESSO (Tulsa, Oklahoma) is an editor with Honor Books. She has been a cheerleader and friend to Ginny and Sherry in the preparation of this book. Sue and her mother, Sarah, are best friends, and they spend many hours together talking, laughing, crying, and sharing dreams. Sue is the mother of one daughter, Lili, whose grand entrance into this world is lovingly shared as one of the many "snippets" of life told in *Seasons of the Heart*.

*Additional copies of this title
are available from your local bookstore.*

Honor Books
Tulsa, Oklahoma